Earth's Riches

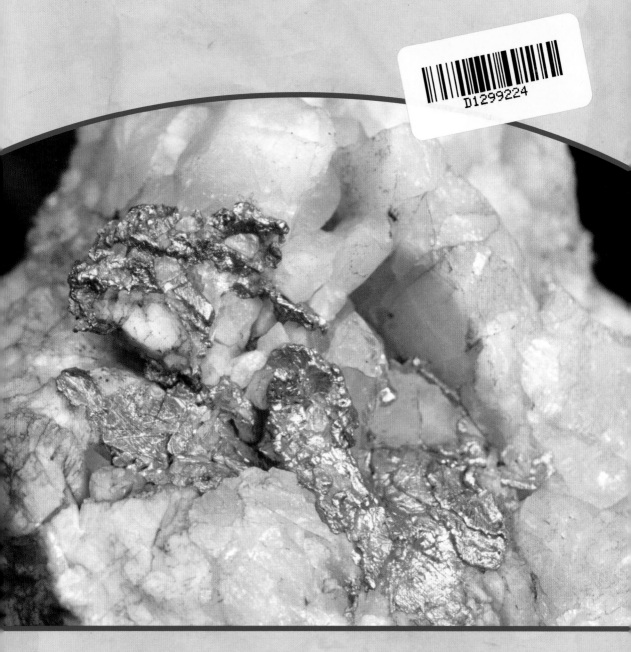

Written by Mary Atkinson

South Africa

My name is Razi. I live in South Africa. My country is famous for its gold and diamonds. Did you know that they are often found under the ground? How do you think people get them out?

Contents

Look for the **Activity Zone!**
When you see this picture, you will find
an activity to try.

Out of the Earth

South Africa is a country rich in gold. It has many other minerals, too. Some, such as diamonds, are beautiful gemstones. Others, such as the metals iron and copper, are used for building things.

Most of the world's gemstones and metals come out of the earth. They are part of the rocks that make up the ground beneath us. People usually get them out by digging large holes.
This is called *mining*.

mineral   a natural substance found in or on the earth

Minerals, Crystals, and Rocks

In 1886, gold was discovered in a small South African farming community. Thousands of people flocked to the area. It is now the busy city of Johannesburg.

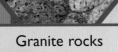

Powdered sulfur

Minerals are solid, natural substances made of basic chemicals called *elements*. Gold, quartz, jade, copper, sulfur, and diamond are different kinds of minerals.

Quartz crystal

A crystal is a mineral that has formed into a regular shape. A diamond is a crystal, and so is a grain of salt.

Granite rocks

Rocks are large, solid lumps of minerals. Many rocks are a mixture of more than one mineral.

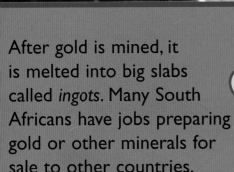

After gold is mined, it is melted into big slabs called *ingots*. Many South Africans have jobs preparing gold or other minerals for sale to other countries.

Mining for Minerals

People have been mining rocks and minerals for thousands of years. There are many types of mines. Some are dug near the earth's surface. Others are deep holes under the ground.

Today, most mining is done by big mining companies. They have huge drills and digging machines that can reach far below the earth's surface. Workers get in and out of the mines by using an elevator. Other elevators bring the minerals up to the surface.

Shaft to bring coal to surface

Layer of coal deep in ground

Many people in South Africa work in coal mines such as this one.

Coal falls into the skip

Conveyor belt moves coal

Cutting machine breaks up coal

This huge hole is part of a diamond mine. The rock has been dug away so that workers can find the diamonds inside it.

Rail cars take coal away

Elevator for miners

Gold is sometimes found in streams as well as underground. People use special dishes to search through the stones in the stream bed.

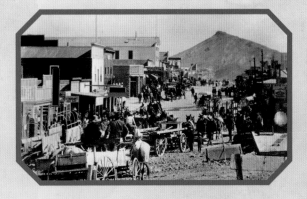

In the 1800s, people rushed anywhere gold was found. This was called a *gold rush*. New towns sprang up almost instantly. Everyone wanted to find a fortune, but only a few actually did.

Precious Metals and Useful Metals

Some of the metals that come from South Africa are worth a great deal of money, because they are rare and beautiful. Gold, silver, and a hard, shiny metal called *platinum* are some of the most expensive metals in the world. They are often used to make jewelry.

Other, more plentiful metals are made into everyday things. For instance, copper is made into pipes and electric wires. Iron is made into steel for bridges, cars, and many other things.

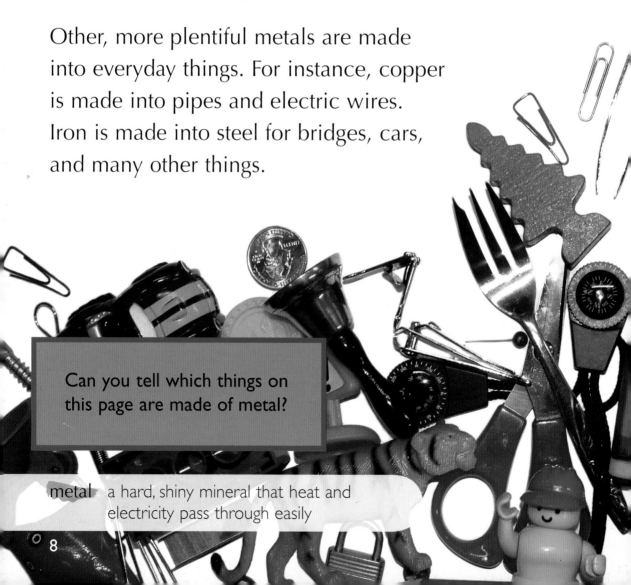

Can you tell which things on this page are made of metal?

metal a hard, shiny mineral that heat and electricity pass through easily

Why Are They Special?

Gold is an expensive metal. Artisans can easily shape it into beautiful objects, because it is soft. It never loses its bright yellow color.

People have been making things out of copper for thousands of years. This bronze bull was made 3,400 years ago.

Silver is a soft but strong metal. It can be bent without snapping. However, over time, it turns a dark color, or tarnishes, and needs to be cleaned.

Platinum looks like silver, but it is harder and never tarnishes. It is difficult to find, which makes it very expensive.

Natural States

When a mineral comes out of the ground, it is not always ready to use. Iron, for example, is often part of another mineral called *hematite*. The iron has to be separated out before it can be used.

Scientists call hematite an iron ore, because it contains iron. Many other minerals are also ores. Galena, for example, is an ore made up of both silver and lead. Before the lead can be used, it has to be separated from the silver.

Azurite

Malachite

Azurite and malachite are both copper ores.

ore   a mineral that is partly made up of something useful, such as a metal

Long ago, people in the Middle East figured out how to get copper out of malachite. They sprinkled bits of malachite on hot coals and blew on the fire to make it hotter. Later, they gathered bits of copper from the ashes.

Galena forms shiny, silver-colored crystals.

From Iron Ore to Steel

Hematite

Limestone

Coke

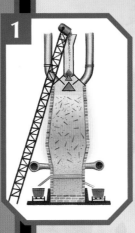

Steel is made using hematite, limestone, and coke.

1. First, the three minerals are put in a huge oven. The heat makes the iron separate out of the hematite and sink to the bottom.

2. The iron is then placed in a different oven, where it is mixed with hot gas. This turns the iron into steel.

3. The hot, melted steel is poured into thin layers. When it cools, it becomes hard.

Glorious Gemstones

Minerals that have formed into large, hard crystals are called *gems*, or *gemstones*. They are rare and difficult to find, which makes them expensive. The best gems are often made into jewelry.

Gemstones come in every color of the rainbow. Different gemstones are found in different countries. Some, such as rubies, let light shine through them—they are *transparent*. Others, such as turquoise, let no light shine through them—they are *opaque*.

Wealthy people in ancient Egypt wore jewelry made from gemstones, just as many people do today.

Today's watches usually have tiny quartz crystals inside them. A crystal helps a watch keep time, because it vibrates at a very even rate when it is connected to electricity from a battery.

vibrate   to move forward and backward very quickly

Gem Cutting

When gemstones come out of the ground, they are often dull and unevenly shaped. Gem cutters cut them into special shapes to make them sparkle. They cut many different surfaces, or *facets*, that catch the light. Here are some ways that gems are cut.

Table cut (ruby)

Emerald cut (emerald)

Round brilliant cut (fire opal)

Pear-shaped brilliant cut (blue topaz)

Heart-shaped brilliant cut (pink topaz)

Cabochon (turquoise)

The Hardest Rock

One of the most valued gemstones is the diamond. It is the hardest mineral on Earth. The only thing that can cut a diamond is another diamond. Some blades, saws, and drills have diamond edges. This allows them to cut almost anything.

Sparkling diamonds are made into expensive jewelry. Large, perfectly formed diamonds are worth a fortune. Most diamonds, however, are tiny.

In the middle of this British crown is a very famous diamond. It even has its own name—the *Koh-i-noor*, which means "mountain of light." Originally, it came from India.

Small diamonds

Koh-i-noor

When diamonds come out of the ground, they do not usually look like sparkling gems. They need to be cut and polished first.

polish to rub something until it is smooth and shiny

Diamonds are too valuable to experiment with, but there are plenty of other crystals you can study.

1. On a piece of black paper, scatter about ¼ teaspoon of raw sugar. Next to it, scatter similar amounts of Epsom salts, rock salt, table salt, white sugar, and bath crystals.

2. Use a magnifying glass to look at the crystals. Compare their sizes, shapes, and colors.

3. Stir a teaspoon of table salt into ¼ cup of water. Pour the water into a saucer and leave it to dry out. What happens to the salt?

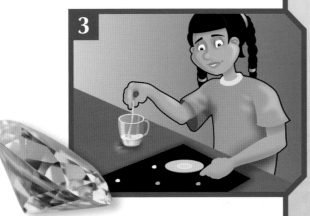

To get one diamond that weighs as much as a pin, miners have to blast out rock weighing as much as about 50 adult people.

15

Taking a Close Look

There are hundreds of different minerals. Some minerals look very similar to other minerals. To tell them apart, scientists check six things:

1. What color is the mineral?
2. Is it shiny or dull?
3. Is it transparent?
4. How heavy is it?
5. How soft or hard is it?
6. What color mark does it leave if you rub it on a white surface?

So many people have mistaken pyrite for gold that it is often called *fool's gold*. Experts know that pyrite is lighter in both color and weight than gold, and it is harder than gold. It leaves a black mark on a white surface; gold leaves a yellow mark.

Scientists who study rocks are called *geologists*. Geologists collect rocks and minerals to find out more about them and the area in which they were found.

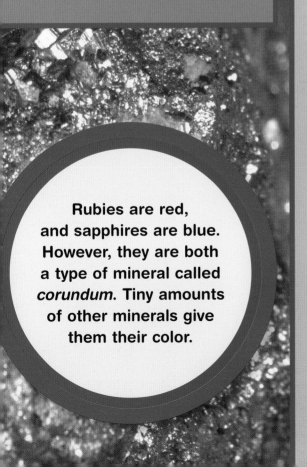

Rubies are red, and sapphires are blue. However, they are both a type of mineral called *corundum*. Tiny amounts of other minerals give them their color.

Mohs' Scale of Hardness

Scientists figure out how hard an unknown mineral is by using Mohs' scale of hardness. The scale goes from one (talc) to ten (diamond). An unknown mineral will scratch only the minerals with a lower rating than itself.

1. Talc—the softest mineral
2. Gypsum
3. Calcite
4. Fluorite
5. Apatite
6. Orthoclase
7. Quartz
8. Topaz
9. Corundum
10. Diamond—the hardest mineral

Rocks, Rocks, Rocks

There are many different kinds of rocks. Some rocks are made up of just one mineral, and others are made up of several different minerals. Granite is made up of the minerals feldspar, quartz, and mica.

Sometimes the minerals in a rock are formed into crystals that are large enough to see. These rocks are called *coarse-grained rocks*. Other times the minerals in a rock form very tiny crystals that are too small to see. These rocks are called *fine-grained rocks*.

Feldspar

Quartz

Mica

Obsidian

Granite

Granite and obsidian are made up of the same minerals. Granite is coarse grained, and obsidian is fine grained.

How Rocks Are Made

Sedimentary Rocks

Some rocks are made when very thick layers of minerals are squashed together under the earth. Limestone is made from the bodies of tiny sea creatures. Their bodies sank, and the hard parts were layered and squashed into rock.

Metamorphic Rocks

When rocks deep in the earth are heated and squashed very hard, they change into different kinds of rocks. When this happens to limestone, it turns into hard, smooth marble.

Igneous Rocks

Some rocks come out of volcanoes as a red-hot liquid called *lava*. The lava cools into hard rock. Scoria is a type of rock that forms in this way.

Clues to the Past

Some rocks tell us about animals or plants that lived long ago. These rocks are called *fossils*. They were formed when bones, shells, or plant parts were buried under heavy layers of mud. Slowly, the mud turned into stone. Minerals replaced the plant or animal parts, turning them into stone, too.

Scientists use fossils to find out about dinosaurs and other creatures that are now **extinct**. First they dig the fossils out of the surrounding rock. Then they study the fossils to figure out what the animals were like when they were alive.

This is a fossil of a *Lystrosaurus*. It was a sheep-sized creature that lived in South Africa more than 220 million years ago.

extinct when a plant or animal no longer exists because it has died out

Scientists use small digging tools and brushes to remove a fossil from the ground. They must be careful not to break it.

From Bone to Stone

When an animal dies, its soft parts are the first to rot away. The hard parts, such as the bones, are left behind.

Sometimes the bones are covered up before they can rot. As layers of sand or mud build up, the layer with the bones is squashed into rock.

In time, the bones rot, leaving a bone-shaped hole. Minerals in the ground water fill the hole and slowly form into a hard, bone-shaped rock.

When mud turns to stone, it sometimes keeps its shape. For instance, these footprints made in mud can still be seen in the stone millions of years later.

21

A View to the Future

Mines do not last forever. Sooner or later, the minerals in a mine run out. Sometimes new mines are dug nearby. Other times, scientists figure out ways to dig even deeper to reach more minerals. However, it is becoming harder and harder to find large supplies of many minerals.

One way we can help is by using things more than once. Old cans and bottles can be melted down and made into new ones. This is called *recycling*.

These squashed aluminum drink cans are ready to be recycled.

This playground slide is made out of recycled plastic. The soft ground covering is made from recycled car tires.

Energy Choices

Oil, coal, and gas come from under the ground. Unfortunately, the world's supplies are getting lower. Sharing cars and not wasting electricity are ways that we can help make our fuel supplies last longer.

These windmills convert wind power into electricity. This is called *wind farming*. Wind energy is renewable and does not cause pollution.

Recycled aluminum cans can be made into any shape. They can be made into pipes, aluminum foil, or more drink cans.

fuel   something that is burned to give heat or to power machines

23

Find Out More!

1 What kinds of minerals are found near where you live? Are any metal ores or gems found in your state?

2 What different things can people do to save Earth's minerals?

To find out more about the ideas in *Earth's Riches*, visit **www.researchit.org** on the web.

Index